UNSTUCK

RUN THE BUSINESS
DON'T LET IT RUN YOU

Phil Duke

Daniel Gomez Enterprises, LLC

UNSTUCK
Run the Business, Don't Let it Run You
Written by Phil Duke

Published by Daniel Gomez Enterprises LLC / May, 2024
Contact Info: (210) 663-5954
Email: Info@DanielGomezGlobal.com

Copyright © 2024, Phil Duke. All rights reserved.
ISBN: 9798326577207

No part of this book may be used or reproduced by any means, graphic, electronic, or mechanical, including photocopying, recording, taping or by any information storage retrieval system without the express written permission of the author except in the case of brief quotations or except as permitted by U.S. copyright law.

The content is the sole expression and opinion of its author. No warranties or guarantees are expressed or implied by the content herein.

Dedication

This book is dedicated to God.

Table of Contents

Introduction   *i*

Chapter 1
Hearing What Hurts – Truth   *p. 1*

Chapter 2
The Danger of Staying Small   *p. 7*

Chapter 3
Road Maps   *p. 13*

Chapter 4
Building the Model   *p. 25*

Chapter 5
Who to Hire First?   *p. 31*

Chapter 6
Recruiting Solves Everything   *p. 37*

Chapter 7
Accountability –The Secret Ingredient   *p. 43*

Chapter 8
Retention Matters   *p. 49*

Chapter 9
Scaling the Business   *p. 55*

Chapter 10
What's Next?   *p. 61*

Introduction

Thank you so much for purchasing this book. I hope it helps you along the way.

In this book, I share my story of how I got myself unstuck. Like many of you, I got into business for myself to experience freedom— freedom of time, location, and income. In the beginning of my business journey, I was simply trying to make a living. Once I started experiencing success, I realized I had to start conducting business differently.

I experienced a great amount of success in the real estate industry. I was selling a lot of houses, making a lot of money, and winning a lot of awards. But I felt stuck. I realized that I did not truly have a business, because a business is something that can operate, function, and grow without you having to be there every single day. I looked around and realized a lot of other "successful" people in the real estate industry were basically doing the same things that they were doing five, ten, or even twenty years ago. They were exchanging time for money. The only way they could make more money, was to simply continue to go out and sell and do so more efficiently and at higher levels than they had ever done before. I realized I had a job instead of a business—a high paying job, but a job nonetheless.

So, I became obsessed with the idea of creating a business for myself, something that could operate, function, and grow without me having to be there every single day. Some of the things I did along the way actually got me even more stuck than I was before. I made a lot of mistakes along the way. There were things I had to learn that I didn't know I had to learn. This book will not give you every single little detail that you need to go from being a solopreneur to an entrepreneur, but it will provide many basic lessons that I wish I had learned sooner.

My hope is that this book becomes a cheat code for you on your journey. I hope that it saves you time and money, and I hope that you share some of the lessons you've learned along the way with others as those situations present themselves.

If you like the content of this book and the idea of becoming unstuck, I would love to connect with you. If you look me up on social media, you will find links to free trainings that I host every single week. I would love to see you on one of those and help you become unstuck.

Phil Duke Jr.

Chapter 1

Hearing What Hurts - Truth

A brain surgeon makes a lot of money for what he does, right? He may have his name on the office door. He might have his name on the business license. He may have business insurance. He may have a manager. But most brain surgeons don't really have a business.

The brain surgeon makes great money as long as he is in the operating room performing surgeries. But if he decides to take a break; decides to slow down a bit, if he has a family emergency or has an emergency himself, health issues, or experiences burnout, his income goes down the moment he takes his foot off the gas.

The brain surgeon does not have a business. He has a high paying job. This is what we often see across the business entrepreneurship landscape. We find people who are high wage earners who call themselves entrepreneurs and business owners. But if we look at their business under a microscope, we would find that they simply have a job - although it may be a very high paying job, but it is still a job nonetheless.

So, what do most entrepreneurs try to do? They are stuck in this cycle of show up, produce, bring in revenue, repeat. We often see that the high wage earner tries to figure out how to produce more, how to produce more efficiently, how to scale things through automation, how to hire people to take some of that admin stuff off of their plates so they can spend more time in the operating room.

There is nothing that you are currently doing in your business that can't be done by someone else. Read that again. If you are stuck right now in your business and you feel like you cannot get out of this never-ending cycle of show up, produce, bring in revenue, repeat, then the first step is realizing that you are stuck in a cycle. We all get stuck at different times in our careers. You may be at the height of your career when you are reading this book. When I was at the height of my career as a top producing real estate agent, I was making more money than I had ever made. I was selling more houses than I had ever sold before. Everybody in the world was telling me how good of a job that I was doing but I felt more stuck than ever! I could not sit at the table and have dinner with my family without taking phone calls. I could not go on vacation without working deals.

> *There is nothing that you are currently doing in your business that can't be done by someone else.*

Realizing that you are stuck is the first step. Realizing that you have A high paying job instead of a business is the first step in this process. You may not believe that right now but there truly is nothing going on in your business today that can't be done by somebody else.

Your business is not the logo. Your business is not the branding. The business is not you necessarily, even though you may be the figurehead of the business. Your business is the collection of systems and processes that you and your employees follow.

You do not even have to be the best in your town, in your state or in the country. You just have to be duplicatable. This may be contrary to what you currently believe but I want to share an example with you. Think about McDonald's hamburgers. If you can cook at all, you can probably go to the grocery store today and buy some hamburger meat. You can marinate it, put some seasoning on it and you can go home tonight and cook a burger that's going to be better than anything on the McDonald's menu.

McDonald's is not trying to have the best hamburgers in the world. If you were making a list of the top 10 hamburgers in the country, McDonald's would not be in the top 10 but yet they are selling an average of 6.5 million hamburgers every single day and they largely follow the same pattern. They cook them the same way, they look the same way, they smell the same way, regardless of whether you go to McDonalds in Tuscaloosa, Alabama where I live or in Nashville, Tennessee or in Chicago, Illinois. You are pretty much getting the same McDonald's hamburger everywhere you go.

Speaking of hamburgers, let me give you this example. Let's say that you are the best hamburger cook in the world. Everybody loves your burgers. You have a wildly successful restaurant and the seats are packed every single day. After all your bills are paid, after all the employees are paid, let's say that your restaurant is making $25,000 per month in net profit. But because you're the best hamburger cook in the world, and nobody else can cook them like you, you have got to be at the restaurant cooking hamburgers seven days a week.

What if you took the time to write out your process, your recipe, and your system? Then you could teach other people how to cook hamburgers. Then you could open up a second location, a third location, or a tenth location. You are going to give up some profit as you grow this business. You will always give up profit for the sake of a more scalable business. Let's say you only make $2,000 per month on these new locations instead of $25,000 like you were on the original location? Would you do that? $25,000 with you running everything versus $2,000 per month and you are not doing anything anymore?

How many locations could you have if you were not involved in any of the day-to-day operations? You could have a lot, right? 12 locations at $2,000 per month gets you to $24,000 per month without you getting tied to the daily operations. Because you're not tied into those daily operations, you can keep going to 15 locations, 20, 100, 1000 locations. But you have got to have a business that can be duplicatable by somebody else.

Staying with the restaurant example, is your business going to be a 5-star restaurant or a Chick-fil-A? A five-star restaurant requires a five-star Chef to be there. What happens when the five-star Chef leaves? The business has to take a break. They have to go find another five-star Chef. They might have to close temporarily. They might have to close permanently.

Be careful about building your business model around highly skilled people. Look at how Chick-fil-A does their business. They take teenagers off the street with no experience cooking and no culinary degree and they cook that Chick-fil-A chicken the same way at every location I've ever been to. I do not have a favorite cook at Chick-Fil-A. When I pull up to the drive-thru I don't ask who is cooking today. No matter who's cooking today, it tastes the same.

Be careful about building your business model around highly skilled people.

You might not have thought about business in that way before, and that's okay. You may have thought business was about intense self-development, 3:30 a.m. wake ups, (and you can't wake up at 3:30 in the morning without posting about it on social media, right?!) working 16- and 18- hour days. I used to be impressed by that.

I used to want to figure out how I could get more efficient and more productive. That certainly is part of the process. You will have to figure out ways of being more efficient and productive but if you really truly have a business and you truly are an entrepreneur, your job is to not have a job. What I mean by that is that you figure out the model, you then map out the model and what the different roles are going to be. Then you map out how people are to do those different roles and you personally don't have to fulfill those roles yourself. You just have to make sure that someone is fulfilling those roles.

For me in the real estate industry, it looked something like this. I would hire a new agent and someone would help onboard those people. I also had someone recruiting those people in. The recruiter recruits the agent, the onboarding specialist onboards them. We pair them up with a mentor inside the office who also got paid on every transaction that that new person did the entire time they were with us.

Once they got properties under contract, a closing coordinator stepped in and would help them do all the paperwork. We weren't having to rely on high-performing people who always did their paperwork right. We got transaction coordinators to do that. Then we had an accounting team that when we did closings, they would pay out to the agent the commission that belonged to them. They would pay out to the mentor what belonged to them and they paid out to the office what belonged to them. It's done the same way at every location.

I am not the transaction coordinator. I was a recruiter for a little bit until I built it up to where I could hire a recruiter. The goal is to eventually get to a place where you don't have a job, meaning you don't have a role to fulfill every day. Get to a place where nobody is depending on you to show up to the office and get things done. The business does not slow down because of you. The business doesn't really speed up because of you, either. It is its own living and breathing organization.

You can certainly provide input and provide guidance. But this thing needs to run without you if you're ever truly going to have a business that allows you to not have a job.

We want to have a business that can run without you and can grow without you, a business that can create cash flow without you. It all starts with realizing that even though you may not truly have a business today, there are some steps that you will learn in this book that you can take today and this month and this quarter and this year to get to the point where you are truly an entrepreneur and you don't have to have a job.

This book will walk you through how I went from being a top producing real estate agent to today, having 10 locations across six different states. I am not on the lease of any of those locations. I am not approving the payroll anywhere. We built a system and I oversee the system. I coach and train the leaders that are running those locations and that is the extent of my involvement today.

It took years to get there. I could have done it a lot sooner knowing what I know now. I wrote this book hoping to share with you what I went through to get there. These are the steps that I took and am taking in other businesses that I am involved in to get to that point faster. I want to help you get unstuck.

Chapter 2

The Danger of Staying Small

When I started having some success as a real estate agent, I got into rental properties. I really had no clue what I was doing. I didn't really do any research at all. I didn't have a great plan going into it. But over the course of several months, I ended up purchasing three rental properties. I put as little money down as possible. I had tenants in there, nothing was tearing up and rent was coming in every month. It was a good thing. I thought, *"Man, I have made it!"*

Until one of my tenants unexpectedly decided to move out. Then the air conditioner at another one of the properties tore up and I had to replace that. I went from having a business that was pretty hands-off and running smoothly to having two of my units vacant and one of them needing repairs out of my pocket.

It is dangerous being small. Listen to me. It is dangerous having a small business. I went from having three properties that were paying me money to all of a sudden having to pay mortgage payments and maintenance. Looking back on it now, I should have been better prepared going into it.

I didn't know what I did not know.

The same thing happens if you have a very small business. Let's say you have the best 5-person business out there in the world. But then you lose one or two of your key players from that business. Losing two of your five is a 40% loss to your business and that might be enough for you to say, "Things were better off when I was just solo" or "Things were better when it was just me doing my own thing."

> *I didn't know what I did not know.*

I see business owners going through this cycle over and over again. They stay small because they think it's going to be easier to manage. They think it's going to be better, less stressful. and after a period of time, it is just not profitable enough for them to sustain the business. They end up reverting back to what they were doing before which is more than likely doing everything all by themselves.

I want to talk about some of the dangers of staying small. One danger is that you never have enough business coming in to justify hiring people to help you run this business. You stay small, you stay manageable and you can handle everything yourself. So, what ends up happening? You end up running everything yourself.

When you do not hire a bookkeeper to manage your bank accounts, guess who the bookkeeper is? You are! When you don't hire a cleaner to clean your office (because it only takes you 30 minutes per week) guess who the office cleaner is. It's you!

The reality is you cannot save your way to prosperity. If you are reading or listening to this book, it is likely that your skill set is on the entrepreneurial side of the spectrum. You may be in sales, marketing, being a visionary or putting systems together. If you are not careful, you end up just doing what has to be done day-to-day to keep the business afloat because you are the only one there who is responsible for doing that.

You have always done it that way. You've always done it yourself. You did it that way because you were able to. You did it that way because you were available. This might be reviewing payroll, onboarding or training new hires that come into your business, it might be general office administrative work, or running to the bank 2 or 3 times a day to deposit checks. It may be preparing or reviewing your profit loss statements.

You cannot save your way into prosperity.

Sometimes what happens in these scenarios is that you end up putting fires out all day, every day. You end up taking phone calls all day like you are some kind of 24/7 help desk. This begins to chip away at your core competency, which is more than likely in sales, marketing, systems, and on the visionary side of things.

You likely began this business to spend more time doing things you felt like you were very good at. But now because you have to handle all these other things that nobody sees, it can slowly start to chip away at you. It starts slowing you down. Your productivity goes down. Now you are not only doing what you were already doing but now you have to add all of these new tasks. It can be a hard cycle to break out of when your business stays small and manageable.

Now, small might seem more manageable. You may be thinking to yourself, "It may be easier to manage this business if I keep it small." That is exactly where I was along with almost everybody I have ever coached or trained or talked to about starting a business. This is where their initial mindset is. "Let me keep this small and manageable. I'll hire really good people that I don't have to manage and babysit. I don't want the headache of managing a bunch of people." And you would be right in some aspects but let me tell you a secret.

Having a larger, more profitable business is actually easier to run than a small business. In fact, it's not even close. I've done both. The hardest but part of growing my first real estate company was when I went from two people to 15 people. At that point, I had all these extra duties and responsibilities but I did not have enough money coming in yet to really hire people to help me run the business.

My first real estate company got much easier to manage after I grew to 25 agents. When it was small, I was doing everything. And I mean every little thing. I was doing the recruiting. I would then train the agents that we would hire. I would answer their phone calls when they were out in the field and needed help. I would review their files because I was also the qualifying broker which meant my license was on the line if they messed up. I was making trips to the bank, writing out commission checks, reviewing the bank statements, preparing the profit and loss report on QuickBooks even though I did not have any idea what I was doing with QuickBooks. I was vacuuming the office, buying office supplies and stocking the refrigerator. It wasn't that I could not do those things, it just didn't really make sense for somebody with my skill set to be taking care of office administration duties for part of the day.

You see, when your business is big and profitable, you can hire people to help run it for you. It also doesn't sting as bad if somebody walks away from that business. In the rental portfolio example I gave earlier, things were going well when all three of my rental properties were paying rent on time and nothing was breaking. But when one property went vacant and the other one had maintenance issues, all of a sudden these were much bigger hits. I was in the danger zone and didn't know it.

If I would have had 20 or 30 rental properties and had one or two vacancies and one or two that had maintenance issues, I still would have had a bunch of other properties generating income that were not giving me issues. I hate it anytime we lose an employee. But the bigger my business got, it didn't hurt so bad when one or two would walk out the door because I had anywhere from 50 to 80+ more behind them that stayed.

When your business is big and profitable you can hire people to run it for you. When you are small and doing everything yourself and keeping the profit to yourself, there may not be enough money to go around.

What if your business was generating a monthly profit of $100,000 per month after all the bills were paid? That would be a good place to be in, right? You could hire people to help you get there. The crazy thing about this concept is that so many people start off their business where they are doing everything with plans of eventually being profitable enough that they can hire help. Unfortunately, sometimes, they never get out of that cycle.

There are people out there who love to do those things that are bogging you down and they are probably better at it than you are. They are out there hoping that somebody like you would offer them an opportunity to manage, to administrate. They probably could not do what you are doing on the sales and marketing front.

Remember the goal of an entrepreneur is to not have a job. The only way to not have a job is to take every single task that is critical to running your business and have somebody else handle that task. The only way to become an entrepreneur instead of a solopreneur is to get other people involved. This is hard to do if the business stays small. There is just not enough money to go around. That is why you have to go big. Being a bigger business frees you up to spend more time doing what you enjoy doing most.

> *Remember the goal of an entrepreneur is to not have a job.*

It is hard to get clarity on what your business needs when you are stuck inside that business running the day-to-day tasks instead of looking at it from an outsider's point of view. If you are not careful, you will start this business and you will do everything yourself. While it is a valid way of growing a business, some people struggle with growing the business and running the business at the same time. It is something to be aware of and understand how dangerous it is.

The big takeaway I want you to remember from this chapter is that staying small puts you in the danger zone. Going bigger becomes easier and actually protects you more from employees walking out the door, accounts walking out of the door and the business shifting. When your business is bigger it is easier to weather the storms.

Staying small puts you in the danger zone.

Chapter 3

Road Maps

There are three main road maps that people can use to get themselves out of being stuck. There are a lot of people out there today who like talking about the concept of getting themselves out of production. That means that they are no longer producing, or selling. They are no longer out there hustling and grinding the way they were maybe three, four, or five years ago. There is a path that goes beyond, one where you are not only not involved in the production of your business, but you're not involved in the day-to-day operations of your business.

I want to cover three main road maps that people can use to get themselves out of production first and then, second, out of the daily operations.

- The Exit Plan Road Map
- The Side Hustle Road Map
- The Investor Path Road Map

The Exit Plan Road Map

In this book, I'm going to spend more time talking about the Exit Plan Roadmap. I think that is where most people naturally try to go in the beginning. It makes sense, it is safer and they are building the business around themselves as a producer, and as the main revenue generator. With this road map, you will slowly start delegating tasks. You'll be hiring people and outsourcing tasks that slow you down until you eventually get to the point where you only have two or three main tasks that you are responsible for in your business.

I'm going to share this from the lens of how this path worked for me as a real estate professional. I know that people are reading this book who are not in the real estate business. I want you to think about how you can take some of these concepts that I used on the Exit Plan Road Map and apply them to your business.

Before I get into the details of this road map, I will say that this road map is probably the hardest one of the three. But it is also the safest of the three. You can always revert to being a solo salesman, a solo producer, a solo physician, etc. We see a lot of people have that "entrepreneur seizure" as Michael Gerber refers to it in his book, *E-Myth Revisited*. Honestly, it is probably not the best path but I think it is the one that most people will use so that is what we are going to spend most of the time in this chapter talking about.

The Exit Plan Road Map

1. The Exit Plan Road Map is a concept where you start by delegating your non-money-making activities. If you are an entrepreneur, business owner, or producer, you more than likely have things that you are responsible for in your daily, weekly, and monthly business cycle that slow you down from getting out there and

> *Start by delegating your non-money-making activities.*

producing more revenue for your business.

It might be running errands, reviewing bank statements, cleaning the office, buying office supplies, etc. It could be things in your personal life that you can only do on your days off like getting your car cleaned up, getting your grass cut, or getting your oil changed. These are all non-money-making activities but they are also essential activities that have to happen inside of a business.

Delegating the non-money-making activities in today's day and age with the internet and people being connected all over the earth, is very easy. Find somebody to handle your QuickBooks for you. It's easy to find somebody who could come and cut your grass every two weeks. With online bill pay, you can set it up to where they receive payment every two weeks. Set it up one time and you can forget it. There are even services that will come to your office while you are prospecting, while you are out generating leads, while you are seeing customers. They can change your oil while your vehicle is parked in your parking lot. I even have a guy here who not only changes my oil but rotates my tires while I am doing other things. That is step number one on the Exit Plan Road Map: delegate the non-money-making activities.

2. The second part of the Exit Plan Road Map is to delegate the money-making activities that take up most of your time. For me, as a real estate agent, that was showing houses. If you are not in the real estate business, you may think that showing houses is super fun and exciting. You get to go see all these beautiful houses! I would say that, in the beginning, it is kind of fun. But the longer you do it, the more you realize that it is a huge waste of your time that could easily be done by somebody else.

For example, you might have a Saturday morning showing at 10:00 a.m. You get there at 9:50 a.m., open up the blinds, and turn all the lights on. Your buyer that wanted to see the house at 10:00 a.m. comes running in at 10:40. Or they might be there when you arrive at 9:50 a.m. and they want to spend over an hour looking at one house. Showing houses is a money-making activity for a real estate professional but it is a money-making activity that takes up a lot of time. There is no guarantee that if we show houses to somebody today, we are going to find them a house that would meet their needs and that they would feel comfortable and confident in going ahead and placing an offer on. For me, delegating the money-making activities that were taking up a lot of my time included simply having some other agents who could handle showings for me.

And I found that even though I was not physically there in person anymore, the buyers were still able to find the kitchens without me. They were still able to find the toilets. They were still able to find the entrances and the exits. They were still able to find the garage. I didn't necessarily have to be there! It only takes a small amount of specialized skill to show the house. The true skill was getting that customer to want me to be the agent that was going to be handling their transaction. They had hundreds of agents to pick from, and I was great at explaining my process for helping home buyers through the process. I focused solely on doing that job and let someone else go out and show them the houses they wanted to see. So, while the showings were happening (and sometimes it was two or three different people that were out at the same time with different showing agents who were doing the showings for me), I could be spending more of my time in the office, in the conference room, at the coffee shop, at a kitchen table finding a new customer instead of out there showing houses to a customer that we already had.

Think about what activities make money for you but take up a lot of your time. Think about when you go into a doctor's office. The doctor is usually not the one taking your blood pressure or temperature. They are not putting you on the scale or asking you what type of symptoms you have. They have a nurse or a nurse's assistant who usually handles those things for the doctor. This way, the doctor can just go from room to room, and spend as little time as possible (from my experience) inside the room seeing the patient. They're not getting themselves bogged down by things that are slowing them down. They can be more efficient by delegating some of those activities.

3. The third step on the Exit Plan Road Map is to focus on activities that pay you 50x instead of 1x. I want you to remember the number 50. Not only did these agents help me with the buyers I had given to them, but I was also teaching them along the way to find their own buyers and their own sellers. I got paid on the ones that I was giving to them, those that they were going out and showing houses to my clients. But I was also helping them find their own clients and also getting paid a little bit for every one of those that they found. Instead of selling a house and getting paid once, I could hire an agent and I could get paid every time that agent had a closing. Potentially, for years and years and years. People are still working in some of my locations right now who have been with me since this thing started in 2018. They are still with me today.

Focus on 50x instead of 1x.

I stopped working on things that only paid me once and I started only spending my time on things that could provide at least 50 pay days to my business. This might be hiring a salesperson or locking down some type of recurring account. It might be a corporate account or corporate contract, or it could be creating an onboarding system for new hires. If I created a good onboarding system, which ours is an online course that I created that every person we hire goes through that online course, I created that course one time and now every single person we hire gets the same training, the same information and they can go back to it over and over again. That is a 50x return right there!

The biggest return that you will ever make is hiring somebody who can handle sales for you. And for you, it might not be a salesperson. It could be a revenue generator. If I had an HVAC company, I would want to have technicians who can handle customers, who can go out and diagnose issues that were going on at a customer's house, and also sell them on a maintenance plan. If I were a dentist, I would want as many dentists working for me as possible who could bring in revenue to the business. But for most people out there hiring a salesperson is going to be the best use of your time. Hiring a recruiter to hire the salespersons would also be a great use of your time.

At this point (step number three), I was no longer selling real estate anymore. I had moved into a role where I was the one coaching, training, and recruiting. Because I had moved to number three, I was only focusing on activities that were going to pay me a 50x instead of a 1x.

I thought this was the best thing ever! I had gotten out of selling. I wasn't out there working the crazy hours that I had been before as a top-performing real estate professional. But what I realized was that I still had a job. It was just a different job. I went from finding buyers and sellers to now I was finding real estate agents. I was coaching them. I was on-boarding them. I was mentoring them. And that took up a great deal of my time as well. I was good at it. I had agents from other companies who I started coaching. I would coach them better than their current brokerage firm was coaching them and they would naturally come over to my company because they saw that I could make an impact for them.

I realized that I still had a job. I was not unstuck at this point. I had gotten down to where all I was doing at this point was recruiting, onboarding, training, and mentoring the folks that I was bringing in.

4. Step number four on the Exit Plan Road Map is to hire a manager. Now that I had a lot more salespeople in our organization, we had a lot more sales coming in which also meant a lot more revenue added to the business. Now that I had that influx of revenue coming in monthly from all of those new money-making team members that I had hired, I decided to invest some of that money into hiring a manager.

I still had a job. I was not unstuck at this point.

I went from working with buyers and sellers as an agent to hiring agents who would work with buyers and sellers in a recruiter/trainer-type role. Then I hired a manager who would hire and train the agents so those agents could go out and work with the buyers and the sellers. So instead of spending my time recruiting and training the money-making team members, my job now became training and coaching my manager. I did this for only 1 hour most weeks. Not only had I moved out of a production role as an agent, I had now moved totally out of the day-to-day operations of my business by hiring a manager. I thought this was the best thing ever as well until I found step number five.

5. Step number five is to expand the business. Once you have gotten out of production and out of the daily operations, you have got to be careful to avoid the temptation to get yourself back into another job again. This was tempting for me. I had the confidence at that point and thought to myself, *I know how to grow a business.* Over a few years, I went all the way through the Exit Plan Road Map and got myself out of the day-to-day with a manager in place running my business. It was tempting for me to go to the next town over, which would have been Birmingham Alabama for me, and start over from the beginning. I paused and I had to get clarity. Did I want to jump back into a job again? I kind of liked this new life that I had. I had all these options now, all this time on my hands.

What I chose to do, which is exactly what I would recommend for you to do when you get to step number five, is to take a portion of your profit from this new self-managing business and use some of that profit to simply fund your new business venture. Be the money person, don't be the worker bee. Every business has a money person and a worker bee. Sometimes it is the same person in both roles.

Once you have gotten yourself out of the day-to-day production, and out of the day-to-day operations, the goal is to not get back into that position ever again. Think about the Sharks on the show *Shark Tank*. They will say something like "I will give you $300,000 in exchange for 30% equity in your company." They are not saying they are going to show up and open up the office for you or come in and be a salesman for you. They are not volunteering to train people for you. They use their knowledge, skills, abilities, relationships, and networks to help these businesses expand faster than they ever thought possible. But they are not signing themselves up for more work.

When it comes to expansion, there is horizontal integration and there is vertical integration. Vertical integration is where you go up and down the supply chain. Explore the things that come before you and after you in the supply chain. Then you go out and try to acquire some of those types of businesses.

Horizontal integration is when you find people who are doing basically the same thing that you are doing and you figure out how to acquire them. That certainly is an option as well. For me, in the real estate profession, since recruiting salespeople was such a big part of the success of my location, I thought, "Why don't I partner with a real estate school?" At first, I thought about starting a real estate school. But knowing what I know today, instead of starting things from the beginning I tried to look for people who are already doing these things. Then I try to figure out how to become a small percentage owner of what they are doing in exchange for helping them expand.

I get 35% of every course that sells because I partnered with an existing real estate school. We were already sending people to real estate school anyway so they could come work for us. It just made sense to create a partnership with a real estate school. Instead of trying to figure out how to do it on my own, or learning about what it took to start a school on my own, I found a real estate school that was already open and wanted to grow and expand. We created a deal that was a great benefit for them and a great benefit for us. That might be something for you to think about. I would try to avoid doing a startup ever again if I could avoid it. Instead, find somebody who is already doing these things and figure out how you can become some type of a partner with them.

Mortgage is the same thing in real estate. Every buyer that we work with has to get a mortgage unless they are going to be paying cash. Wouldn't it make sense, if we are already going to be using a mortgage company anyway, to be using a mortgage company that we are part owners of?

Find somebody already doing these things and partner with them.

It is the same thing with title companies. Every house that we close on involves a title company. Wouldn't it make sense that if we are going to close with a title company anyway, to close with a title company that we are part owners of?

I want you to understand that you do not have to know how to run a mortgage company. You do not have to run a real estate school. You do not have to have a license to be an instructor and teach the real estate school. I would start from day one not being in any of those day-to-day roles in your business. You have worked hard to get out of the day-to-day production and out of the day-to-day operations of your business.

That is the Exit Plan Road Map. You start largely on your own, maybe with a few helpers here and there. You try and grow the business and gradually start peeling yourself more and more away from the day-to-day activities until it is to the point that it is profitable enough for you to put a manager in place to run that business for you. It seems like that is the road map that most people go with naturally anyway. But I will tell you, it is also the one that will be the toughest. There are going to be times when you feel like you want to give up. There are times when your brain is going to tell you something like *Life was easier when we didn't have all these people. Why don't I just go back to being a real estate agent and not have to deal with an office, or not have to deal with agents?*

I want you to think about a cow versus a bison. When a storm is coming, a cow lays down. They simply lay down and wait for the storm to pass over. They get rained on. They are lying in the thunder and lightning for a long time. That has got to be tough. The bison, however, sees the storm and they run towards it. They run right through the storm. It is still tough but only for a little bit. Because they are putting their head down and running headlong into the storm, it is quicker for them to get through that storm.

This is the best advice that I can give you for this Exit Plan Road Map. It is going to be tough. It is going to be a lot of work if things go right and you stick to the plan. If you put your head down and are 100% committed, you can come out on the other side of this thing and never go back into production or the daily operations of your business ever again.

The Side Hustle Road Map

The second is the Side Hustle Road Map. This is where you keep doing what you are doing if it is highly profitable and easy. Maybe you do not want to deal with a bunch of employees, hiring and training, onboarding, etc. You are going

Keep doing what you are doing if it is highly profitable and easy.

to stick to what you are doing but you are going to also develop some sort of side hustle that is more of a business. If you are the brain surgeon who is making a lot of money or the real estate agent making a lot of money doing what you are doing and you don't want to slow down because you truly enjoy it or you feel like it is very efficient, it may make sense for you to stay in what you are doing but take part of your profit, part of your income that is coming in from that job that you have and develop a side hustle that is truly a business.

The Investor Path Road Map

The third path is the Investor Path Road Map. It is very similar to the side hustle. You are starting on day one not being involved with any of the daily tasks of running the business. You not going to be the one running the business. You are not going to be operating the business. You are not going to be the salesperson. You are just going to take some of your money, find somebody who has a business that is up and going, and become an investor in that business. There will be more to come later in this book about the Investor Path Road Map. The money truly is in the money.

Whichever one of these road maps you end up taking, the goal is to eventually be the investor and not be the day-to-day operations person or the day-to-day production person. We want to be like the shark on *Shark Tank*. We want to put the money in and we want to get a return on that money that was put in there without signing ourselves up for more work, more production, or more operations.

Those are the three road maps. The Exit Plan Road Map is the one that most people are going to go with. It is tough, it is possible, it is doable and I know you can do it.

Chapter 4
Building the Model

If you truly want to get out of the day-to-day operations of producing in your business and eventually out of the day-to-day managing or operating of that business, you have got to have a clear business model.

For most of us who grew up in middle or lower-class families, we have been taught that the path to success is to go out and work hard. We need to produce to close deals and bring in customers, bring in those accounts, and spend more hours working more shifts. Now that does work. Unfortunately, you end up getting stuck doing all of those tasks because there is only one of you.

To have a business that can run and go without you, you have to have a clear road map. Who is going to help you run, operate, and grow this business? Remember, as a true entrepreneur your job should be to not have a job at all. You might be in the beginning part of your business right now where you are doing a bunch of different jobs. Maybe there is not enough business coming in or there are not enough customers. There may not be enough closed deals happening to hire somebody to do every single small task that you are doing right now. But to be a true entrepreneur, we eventually need to get to a point where we are not doing anything involved with the day-to-day business. Eventually, you will motivate your employees, becoming more of a visionary and a figurehead of the business who decides where the future of this thing is going.

Jim Collins briefly speaks about the concept of building your model in his book, *Good to Great*. He mentions getting the right people on the bus, the wrong people off the bus, and then getting the right people into the right seats. To get your creative juices flowing, here is the first question I ask you to consider as you start building your model. How can somebody come work for you and make a lot of money working for you? Can you show them how to make $100,000? Could they stay with you and make a quarter of a million dollars? Could they make $500,000 and beyond? Is there a growth guide that allows for and shows somebody to come in at an entry-level position and move up within your organization? Or are you bringing them into your organization, only to cap out with you so then they must go to a larger organization to continue moving ahead in their career path?

> *How can somebody come work for you and make a lot of money working for you?*

Those people who want to keep moving up are the kind of people that you want to have stick around with your business. if you don't have something in place to allow for that movement, you are going to lose the very best people that you hire.

What does it look like for somebody to come to work for you and make a bunch of money? Do you have that figured out? Could you clearly show somebody multiple paths to six figures by working for you?

What is your business going to look like when it is 10 times bigger than it is today? What additional positions or roles would you need to fill if your business was going to be 10 times bigger than it is today? 10 times bigger could be 10 times more revenue. It could mean 10 times more customers. It could be 10 times the number of employees you currently have. What additional roles would you need to create and fill for your business model to allow that to happen?

What if you had 10 times the locations that you currently have? That could mean 10 locations in one city or locations in 10 different states. It could be a few locations in one region and a few in another region. What roles would you need to fill to run your business if it started to look like that?

Who could help you get there and how would these people be compensated very well for helping your business run, grow, and operate? You have got to remember that you have to make a profit as well. If someone works for you and makes $250,000, are you still winning in that deal? Here are a couple of things I would recommend doing as you are starting this process. Keep in mind, that this is not going to be an overnight process. This is something you're going to have to create a rough draft of and go back to it over and over again. You need to have this model started and in place as early as you can in your business. Write a job description summary for each position or role that you need to fill. Jot down three to five critical tasks that are crucial to that role. For me, the crucial tasks for a manager who is running one of my 1st Class Real Estate offices would be to recruit at least three agents per month, at least one pending sale per month per sales representative and that we have 50% of our listings get a price reduction if they've been on the market for more than 30 days.

Underneath each one of those tasks there would be subtasks that could be created but those are the top three things I would grade my manager on if I had a manager in place. Those three metrics are going to drive that location. If I have a manager who is driving pending sales and getting listings reduced but is not recruiting, then I know I have a problem. I either need to get that person to hit that minimum recruiting number every month or I need to find a new manager.

A sales representative's crucial task list could include one new customer appointment per day. Not one that you have already been working with and are trying to get to the finish line but a true new customer appointment every single day. One new client contract is signed per week. We know that not every contract that gets signed leads to closed business so we are going to give the sales rep a 50% contract signed-to-deal closed ratio so if they are signing one new client per week, we're going to say they need to have at least two deals closed per month.

Mapping this model out and figuring out what drives your business, figuring out the key metrics that you want to follow, the key performance indicators are very important metrics to know for each position. If you do not have it all figured out at the beginning, that is okay. You can do some research, and figure out what has worked at other companies in other Industries but at least get started on building this model.

Lastly, I want to talk about retention. I hear people all over the country complaining about how today's workforce does not have that "Go-Get-It" factor. Business owners complain that they can't find anybody to show up and work. There is a great book out there called *The Dream Manager*. It tells of a custodial cleaning company that hired people to come in and clean offices and houses for approximately $10 an hour. They could not keep people at this company very long. They had about a 60% churn rate within the first 6 months. They would hire people, onboard them, train them, and 60% of those people were no longer with the company after 6 months.

The company began examining what was going wrong. They had

the idea to help people figure out what their dreams were. They had some employees who dreamt of going back to college, or buying a house. Some wanted to get themselves out of debt, or go on a nice vacation. The company came up with a program where a Dream Manager coached their employees to reach towards and achieve those dreams. The workplace became more than just a place to go and collect a check. It became a place where dreams come true.

If you are going to run a business for any length of time, you are going to have people that leave. Guaranteed. You have to have a clear roadmap for someone to come into your company and keep moving up, to keep making more money and to hit new levels to do things that they have been dreaming about their whole lives. If all they have to look forward to is to come in, go to work, and go home you are going to have a hard time keeping people inside your business model.

When you are hiring a $10 an hour person, that $10 an hour person better love that $10 an hour job. If there is no path laid out for them to move up within your organization, they won't stay. It is exciting to see people stay with your organization year after year. I have people running 1st Class Real Estate locations for me today who started off their real estate career from day one and had never sold a house before. Because I had a growth guide, a plan for them to move up to team leader, into an advisor position, into a franchise owner position, I've been able to keep my very best people. These are the people that go above and beyond, those that care about their job. These are the people who want to go to the next level. If you don't have a model to keep those kinds of people, you are going to end up losing your very best people, Year after year and you'll find yourself having to constantly rebuild this business that you have created.

Chapter 5

Who to Hire First?

Your model should be a perfect representation of what your perfect location looks like. It should include roles and responsibilities tasked out for each position.

Now that your model is built, the next step is to start hiring people. As author Jim Collins says in his book, *Good to Great,* "You have got to get the right people on the bus and you've got to get the right people in the right seats." Where do you even start? Who is your first hire going to be?

Many business owners are tempted to hire an administrator, personal assistant or an executive assistant. That is certainly a safe hire but it may not be the best hire for you If you are truly wanting to have a business instead of just a high paying job.

There are two problems with hiring administrative positions. First, these positions don't typically bring in extra revenue. They may take some responsibilities off of your plate which allows you to spend more time on money-making activities, but these employees actually cost you money. They are net-negative to the business.

Especially at the beginning of your business, you need as much money as possible. Almost every entrepreneur or business owner that I've ever talked to has made the comment that it took more time, more energy, and more money than what they had anticipated. In the beginning stages of building your business, you need as much money as possible. Hiring employees that don't bring in extra money to the business eats up much needed cash.

Second, these positions allow you to keep doing more of what you've already been doing, which is bringing in the money. Being a producer, being a closer, and seeing more customers. This is actually taking you further away from being a true business owner. If you have been the one who sells the houses and you bring in an executive assistant to take some of the other stuff off of your plate, you end up spending that extra time selling more houses. That is getting you more stuck than you were before. You just end up even more stuck with a few more sales and a little bit more money than what you had before.

> *Hiring employees that don't bring in extra money to the business eats up much needed cash.*

Hiring admin positions first takes you away from being a true entrepreneur. It actually gets you more stuck than what you were before. You are chasing more sales and chasing more revenue but you're still doing it all yourself. This keeps you in position as the primary revenue generator for your business. That can be a bad thing when you're trying to get out of that cycle. In my opinion, the first hire that you need to make is people who are going to be bringing in additional revenue, profit, and sales for the business.

If you are a dentist, you should be hiring another dentist. If you are in real estate, you should be bringing in other licensed real estate agents. If you work on air conditioners, you should be bringing in other HVAC technicians who can go on appointments, diagnose things and create sales. You need people who can sell and bring in extra money for the business.

You may be asking yourself, why would these people want to work for me? Why wouldn't they just go out and start their own dental office? Why would they not start their own real estate brokerage? Why wouldn't they start their own HVAC company? These people are not worried about building their own business. They just want to do a good job at what they feel like they're good at. They want to be the best professional that they can be. They may want to be you one day but for right now, they just want somebody who can show them the way, who has a proven roadmap to what success looks like in their industry. You may not realize it, but people look up to you when you are a business owner. They may know how hard it is to own a business because they have done it themselves. Or maybe they were scared to open their business and instead they have taken the safe path in life. There are people who are happy just being an employee, working underneath other people. They may have aspirations one day of going out and being in business for themselves but aren't quite ready yet. There are more of these employee-minded people out there in the world than there are people like you who are entrepreneurial-minded. You probably will not have a problem finding people to fill your business model the way that you designed it.

People today are more confused than they have ever been before. There is so much information at our fingertips. We are one Google search, podcast or YouTube video away from becoming an expert on a topic in a matter of minutes. It's called information overload and it paralyzes people. There is a YouTube video, a podcast, or a book somewhere about almost every profession in every industry out there. There's actually a lot of money being made in these coaching spaces that are helping people find clarity and discover their skills to create a vision of what they want for their future.

People are looking for clarity. They are looking for mentors to spend time with them and looking for someone who is going to take a chance on them. That is where you come into the equation. When you hire these people, you are going to spend some time training and developing them. It is going to slow you down. it is going to actually take some revenue off of your plate while you are getting the new person going. I recommend, as you are coaching and training, that you record and document everything you are teaching. If you are giving these classes live, use your phone or laptop to record these training sessions and store them online for future employees to watch.

> *People are looking for clarity.*

I can remember back when I was giving live classes to my real estate agents. We would give four live classes to every single agent that we hired. They had a certain number of tasks that they had to show proficiency in before we would let them go out and show houses let them take leads that we were paying for. In the early days, those classes were recorded simply by opening up my laptop, turning on the webcam and hitting record. We would actually stack the laptop up on books to get it at the right height. There were no professional microphones. Teaching those classes over and over and over gave me a chance to refine my message. I was able to simplify and clarify things that I was teaching to the people that I was bringing on board. I made it a habit to always go back and listen to those recordings of myself. I wanted to critique what I was doing. What sounded good? What sounded confusing? As people had questions along the way, I would write those questions down and add that into those four classes for the next group I was training.

You are going to learn things during this process. If you are truly entrepreneurial minded, you have a skill of taking complex things and simplifying them in a way that makes it easy for you and that, in turn, makes it easy for other people to learn. Don't discount that skill that you have as an entrepreneur.

Come up with three or four main tasks that you want your employees to be proficient in and focus on those fundamental basics over and over. As you are training your current employees, you will also be building the training platform for your future employees. You also may be training people right now who will be training your future employees down the road for you. If you have a systemized process for training a new hire, then training becomes a task that you can pass off to somebody else. These early adopters that come into your business early on often end up being the ones that stick with you for years and years. They are with you in the beginning, helping you build this thing. They go from being trained to doing a little bit of training themselves to being the ones training your new hires for you down the road.

Why hire revenue generating employees? They will make you additional profit. Sure, there will be additional issues that you will have to solve. Your time management and communication skills will have to be developed along the way as a leader. It is very hard to fail in business when you are profitable. Hire people that will help you become more profitable as fast as you can. These people will be the ones bringing in the profit for your business if you ever desire to exit from the revenue generating tasks that you are doing yourself. You might be selling real estate today while also training other people to sell real estate. If you get enough other people selling real estate, you will eventually get to where you are not selling real estate anymore if you wish to exit from production at some point. You own the company that sells real estate but you are not the one out there grinding away, having to schedule days stacked full of appointments one on top of the other trying to figure out how to get more efficient here and there. Hiring revenue generating employees truly is a cheat code to getting yourself out of production and eventually getting yourself out of the day-to-day management of your business.

> *It is very hard to fail in business when you are profitable.*

Chapter 6
Recruiting Solves Everything

We start off by building our model. We figure out what the ideal location looks like, the positions that need to be filled, the skill sets that are needed, and how many people we will need. We have laid out how people will move up within the model. Then we talked about hiring money-making employees. As a new business, we are going to need money so making sure that we hire revenue-generating employees is important.

Now we're going to talk specifically about recruiting money-making employees. What makes a salesperson jump from one organization to the next? You've probably seen an insurance agent jump from one insurance provider to another or you may know a real estate agent who has jumped from one real estate brokerage to another. Have you ever pondered what makes a salesperson switch organizations like that? What makes a W-2 employee jump from their current profession into a totally new industry?

I grew my first location by finding people who weren't even in the real estate business and recruited them. That meant they had to pay for a class, they had to go through a course and study for a state exam. What makes somebody decide to make a big jump like that? It's my opinion that they switch because they believe that a different leader can get them to the next level faster than their current leader. Maybe

> *When they find a leader who they believe can get them to that next level faster, they jump from one organization or industry to the next.*

they have discovered that their current industry is not a good fit for them. Maybe they are having a hard time achieving the income and lifestyle that they desire with their current position. When they find a leader who they believe can get them to that next level faster, they jump from one organization or industry to the next.

Let's talk about how to become that type of leader. Money only motivates people so much. In fact, there are many studies that show that paying employees more than your competitors does not actually result in better employee performance. Sometimes, you end up with people who came for the money but they'll also turn around and leave you for the money when they find somebody offering more or better benefits. We've got to be careful with leading with money. Should money be part of the equation when recruiting? Absolutely! Should it be on par or equal to the industry norm? Absolutely! Better benefits, better leads, better technology are all things that people look at when they are recruiting in the beginning.

Many think they have a better model than their competitors, better technology, better benefits, etc. You have got to be careful recruiting people based on these markers. They may join you for the money but they will also leave you for the money when they find a better deal somewhere else. The same goes with recruiting based on giving them leads. If you recruit people based on the number of leads you have and that all they will have to do is work your leads, but they are struggling with leads where they currently are, they may come join you thinking your leads are better or easier. But they will also leave you when they realize that your leads are no easier to work or convert than the leads at their current place of employment. Be very careful with recruiting using benefits, leads, technology, and money.

People are looking for a leader who can get them to the next level faster than their current leader. What works for me and what seems to work for other people across the country and a variety of industries is coaching your competitors' sales people better than they are. If you start coaching your competitors' agents better than the competitor is coaching them, people will naturally decide to come over. That is what has worked for me. I would invite agents from other real estate agencies into my weekly Mastermind meeting. This is a meeting that we had with all of our sales people every week. It was not a dog and pony show. It was truly for my team but I wanted other agents from other companies to sit in the room and see what it would be like at 1st Class Real Estate. There was no discussion about them moving their license over to my company or getting them to sign anything. I wanted them to take a test drive and see what it would be like to work in my company before they ever even thought about transitioning from their current brokerage over to my brokerage.

When recruiting, ask yourself, do they know who you are and do they know what you do? You might have the best model in the world and you truly might be able to make them more money because of your model, your commission splits, your salary structure and commission structure. But if they don't even know who you are and what you do, then when you make a recruiting call to them, they are just going to see you as just another salesperson. You are no different than the person randomly calling them trying to sell them health insurance or the telemarketers that they're getting robocalls from every day. Do they know who you are? Do they know that you are looking to grow your business? Do they know that you want them to join your team?

Jon Cheplak is a coach and mentor to many top real estate team leaders and brokerage owners across the country. He has a great recruiting script called *The Plan B Script*. This would be step one in recruiting a salesforce over to your organization. The script goes something like this. I'm going to alter it to be specific for the real estate industry:

"Hey, I know you're happy at ABC Realty and you're probably not looking to make a move but I just wanted you to know we would love to be your plan B brokerage over here at Main Street realty."

It is a subtle planting of a seed. It can turn into a recruiting appointment over the next 2 to 3 weeks but it is never going to turn into a meeting or an appointment where you're talking with them about joining your organization if they don't know who you are, what you do or what you are about. If they don't know that you are looking to grow or that you want them, nothing will ever come of it. You see, sales people make moves all the time. Unfortunately, many are not very loyal for the long haul. They are always looking out for what's best for them. The reality of it is, that's how all of us are! We are always looking for the next big thing, the secret pill, the secret formula that is going to make sales easier. We, as the leaders in the room, know that secret pill doesn't exist. But we're always kind of looking for that too if we're being honest.

> *We are always looking for the next big thing, the secret pill, the secret formula that is going to make sales easier.*

We recruited people that weren't even in the industry to come over to our organization using this technique. We would send a text message, a Facebook messenger message, an email, etc. We would say something like, "Have you ever thought about getting into real estate? I think you would crush it..." That's it.

We've had people leave law enforcement jobs and teaching jobs.

We've had stay at home moms come into the business. We have had sales people from other Industries, whether it was insurance or car sales, who thought that real estate might be a way for them to get where they're going a little bit faster. That was an easy way for us to recruit and grow our business. Instead of trying to get existing real estate sales people to come over, we relied more on training people from day one who had never sold real estate before. One of the great things about recruiting inexperienced people is they don't have a lot of bad habits. They have not been taught the wrong way to do real estate. Do you want existing sales people who already have experience? I think the answer should be yes. That is definitely one path you could take. You're going to have to put up with retraining them a bit. You may have to put up with some bad habits. Sometimes you'll have a few divas. Divas think that because they have experience and because they have had success before, they can get away with a little bit more. Those are some of the things you have to deal with when you bring over existing sales people into your industry.

If I could only recruit one type of individual to grow my organization, I would take people who have never been in my industry before and I would coach and train them and get them into production as fast as possible. That has really separated us from the pack as we built our brokerage. We have become the training ground brokerage in town. We are the place to go if you are brand new in real estate and want to get started quickly. We even had other real estate companies in town who did not want to hire brand new people send them over to us because they knew we did a great job training.

Recruiting solves everything. You are going to lose some people no matter how good of a leader you are. You're going to have people who don't do what you teach them and they're going to end up flunking out of the business. It is not going to be your fault. You're going to have people who decide to move to a new area of the country and they may not be able to work for you any longer because of that move. People are going to leave. People are going to make career changes. But if you are constantly recruiting and bringing in the next group of money-making employees, it won't sting as much as if you were losing a top producer and you didn't have anybody coming in the door behind them.

When I was just getting started and my real estate career, I went out and bought three rental properties. I had no clue what I was doing. I had not researched anything about rental Investments nor had I owned investment property before. I just had some extra money and I felt like people that had had success ahead of me had gotten into real estate investing so I did it. It was great when all three of those rentals were paying on time and in good repair. But then one tenant moved out. Another tenant stopped paying. An air conditioner tore up in one unit. All of a sudden, having rentals stinks! It is not a good situation to have two out of three of your units not making any money. But if you had 30 units, it would not sting as bad if two or three were not paying because you'd still have 27 or 28 that were bringing money in for you. That is how we can protect ourselves as we are growing our business.

We hate to lose anybody. It stings anytime somebody leaves but it doesn't sting as much when you know your next group of money-making employees is coming in next week, the next month or the next quarter. That's how recruiting solves everything.

Chapter 7

Accountability: The Secret Ingredient

Now that we have hired some new sales staff, we need to lead and manage these new hires. It does no good to go out and spend time recruiting money-making employees to be part of our organization if they do not end up making us money. You need to have an onboarding system of some sort.

Your onboarding system is going to go over
- your expectations
- your systems
- how to log in to those systems
- how to work those systems
- workflows, how to take a customer from point A to point B to get that deal closed
- calendars and how often you are meeting with your sales staff

It will explain what kinds of meetings and what those meetings will look like. For me, in real estate, I broke my onboarding systems down into four simple things that I wanted them to know. I put all of this information into an online course.

The four things that I wanted them to know were:
1. How to generate leads
2. Hot to conduct a sales appointment
3. How to write offers
4. How to close a deal after it's under contract

I put these four items into an online course format with a skills test at the end once the lessons were completed. This is an 8-hour online training course.

An agent would join our company and we would get them signed up for the online course. They would complete the course at their own pace. Once they were finished with the videos, we would do an in-person skills test where we would have them complete some of these tasks to prove that they had gone through the training. This ensures that they were able to log in to everything and that they knew how to use the systems on a basic beginner level.

Before I go any further, I want to remind you of the 80/20 rule. This rule states that 20% of your sales staff will be responsible for 80% of your production. In real estate, for every ten agents that I would hire, I would get one or two really good agents. I would get three or four average agents and I would get five to six agents that I pretty much couldn't do anything with. I could not get them motivated. I could not get them to show up or take action.

> *The 80/20 rule states that 20% of your sales staff will be responsible for 80% of your production.*

In the beginning, I really thought I could motivate anybody to excel. I thought I could get anybody motivated to the point where they could sell 30+ houses per year, which is absolutely possible for anybody with a real estate license. The problem was, I found out that I can't motivate an unmotivated person. I recommend that as a sales leader, you accept that the 80/20 rule is what it is. Hiring ten agents to get one or two really good ones is just reality. Instead of trying to fix that, accepting that this is just the way it was really helped me scale my business. I wish it wasn't this way but if this is how it is going to be, then I can still win, I can still grow, and I can still be profitable. I just have to accept that this is the game that I'm playing.

Here are some tips to help you deal with the 80/20 rule. Test everybody. Eight hours of online training was required before they could do their in-person skills test. The skills test had to be completed before we would turn their leads on. We had all kinds of online leads that we provided to our agents to try to help them get deals quickly and consistently. If I hired someone on Friday, and it takes them 30 days to finish eight hours of online training, what do you think that tells me about the person I just hired? What if I hired them on Friday and they show up to the office on Monday with all their online training complete and they are ready to take their skills test? Do you think I might coach those two people differently? Do you think I might spend more time with one versus the other? For me, onboarding became a way for me to tell if I was dealing with someone in that 20% category or in that 80% category.

When people show you who they are, it's your job as their leader to recognize and to believe that is who they are. It is not your job to fix them. It is not your job to take an unmotivated person and turn them into a motivated person. Some might not be ready mentally; some may not be emotionally ready or they may have too many other things going on in their personal lives. They may have limiting beliefs that they need to overcome. You let them show you who they are and then lead them accordingly. Build your company around the 20% who are

> *When people show you who they are, it's your job as their leader to recognize and believe that is who they are.*

responsible for 80% of the production.

Now, that may sound a little cold-hearted. In the beginning of this journey, I had a mentor tell me that people who want to be successful will be successful with or without you. At first, I didn't believe that but after 5+ years of leading real estate agents and seeing this play out in real life, I would agree. In the beginning, our onboarding system was nowhere what it is today. Yet we still had people who were successful as real estate sale agents even when our onboarding system was confusing. We still had people who overcame and made it big. If you feel like you are failing people as a sales leader, I want you to realize you cannot fix everybody.

Accountability truly is the missing ingredient. For a while, my business looked like this: We would hire an agent, put them through the onboarding process which was the online course and the skills test. We would let them take that skills test. We would turn on their leads. We asked them to attend our weekly Mastermind meeting in the office. Our Mastermind meeting was the one time every week that we wanted everybody that could be there in the office. Just as a side note, if they say they need or want training and they say they want to make six figures in the first year yet they fail to show up for a one day per week training, what does that tell you? Remember, when people show you who they are, you have got to believe them.

Accountability truly is the missing ingredient.

Since this was the one time per week to get in front of the agents, I felt pressure as the leader to constantly be giving them more value, new ideas, new ways to generate leads and new ways to turn leads into appointments. I would start preparing the agenda for that meeting on Friday. I would make notes and think about it over the weekend. On Sunday afternoons, I would stress out about the fact that I had a group of agents coming in the next morning and I had to figure out some way to get them to take action. I had to help them become successful or else they may end up flunking out of the business. I would conduct these meetings delivering new ideas and they would focus on those new ideas that I shared for a few days. Then they find out that it's not a magic pill to success so they quit doing those things and then they would hear a new idea at the next Monday morning Mastermind meeting. This cycle continued until I realized they didn't actually need new ideas. In fact, the new ideas that I was consistently giving them were actually paralyzing them and distracting them from the basics.

When it comes to your team, which do you think they need more of? More training on new ideas and concepts or having someone hold them accountable to do the things that they've already been trained to do? Which do you think would have a bigger impact on their sales?

I asked this question at one of our weekly Mastermind meetings. They all agreed that accountability is key. They would sell more houses and make more money if they would just do the basics that they had been taught. Instead of constantly trying to learn new techniques and concepts that they were probably only going to incorporate for a short period of time anyway. Accountability really is the secret ingredient for running and managing a profitable sales team.

We created a 30-day step-by-step action plan for all new hires. The plan broke down how many leads needed to go into the CRM every day, how many appointments they needed to be going on every week and how many contracts they needed to get signed during these 30 days. It was simple, basic and kind of boring to be honest. But it works! If you are reading this book, you probably know what it takes for someone to hit their sales numbers. You probably know how many contacts need to be made and how many sales calls need to happen. Break that down and give that to your sales staff as an action plan. Based on that, we developed 30-day, 60-day and 90-day check-ins. At the 30-day mark, they should have one hundred leads entered into their new CRM that they were using at our company. If they did not have one hundred leads when it came to their 30-day check-in, we had a problem. The problem was not that the training was not working, that the market was down or that the interest rates were crazy. The issue wasn't that the market was super competitive. The problem was that this person sitting in front of me was not taking their daily actions. That is a problem worth fixing.

High performers want accountability. That's why many of us end up hiring coaches, going to conferences, paying money to fly across the country to go learn new things. High performers want that. Low performers run from accountability. You have got to decide if you want to build your company around the high performers who want and need accountability or do you want to settle for bringing people in, showing them how to do their job and then sit back and let the low performers be comfortable in their subpar performances. If you can take a mid-level performer and bring them up just a notch, it is a huge win. If you could take a low performer who may be scared or lack confidence and you can get them to take action and go from Level C to level B, that is another huge win for you.

High performers want accountability.

Accountability really is the secret ingredient.

Chapter 8

Retention Matters

No matter what kind of business you are operating or what industry you're in, you are running a sales organization. The brain surgeon is busy with current customers today but he also has to figure out how to fill up the calendar for the next day, the next week, and the next month. Every sale that occurs brings in revenue to the business. By now, hopefully you have created a business model for how all of this is going to operate. You have hired some money-making employees to help your business bring in more money. Side thought: is a receptionist a money-making hire in a brain surgeon's office if that receptionist can book times on the brain surgeon's calendar? Positions you may not have considered to be money-making positions may actually be profitable.

Hopefully things are going well and now you have your team in place. You've got new revenue coming in and everything is going well. Until somebody decides to leave. Sometimes people will leave your organization quickly when they realize they are in the wrong place. They come on board and they quickly determine this is not the right fit. Sometimes people leave because they know they are not holding up their end of the bargain and it's easier for them to go do something else than it is for them to get fired. Sometimes they leave because a recruiter lies to them about how much better it's going to be at another organization across town. And sometimes, people who are in the trenches with you, people who are valued members of the team leave as well. It really stinks when someone leaves your organization, whether they were a big part of your team, a small part of your team or maybe even somebody you are kind of glad to see go. It's not fun. It wasn't what you set out to do when you started this business. It is going to happen regardless of how good you are as a leader or how beneficial of a culture you have created. A certain percentage of people are going to come in and a certain percentage of people are going to leave.

I mentioned back in chapter 6 that recruiting solves everything. Recruiting truly does solve this problem as well. As a business owner, you hate to see anybody leave but it is reality.

Let's imagine that you own three rental properties. In a short span of time, two out of the three become vacant. It really stinks. You bought these properties thinking they were going to pay for themselves. You thought that the tenants were going to pay on time and there was not going to be much required maintenance and needed repairs. Now, all of a sudden, you are having to pay mortgage payments out of your pocket while these units are sitting there vacant. It hurts. It may even make you question if you are cut out to do this rental business or not. But what if you had 30 rental properties and two of them became vacant? It still stings because you are leaving some money on the table, but you have 28 more properties that are still rented and bringing in money for you.

Recruiting solves everything.

Do you see how recruiting can resolve this retention problem? Are you starting to see how staying small like we talked about in Chapter 2 is dangerous and drastically harder than going big? It's way better and safer to have 30 rental properties instead of three. You are going to put a lot of time and energy into recruiting these new people. But you've also got to put time and energy into retaining the folks you already have working for you as well. Here are a few simple things you can do to increase your retention efforts without costing you any money. The whole idea behind increasing your retention rates is to simply make people feel valuable.

Here are a few things I have done over the years to help people feel valuable.

1. We do a Monday morning Mastermind meeting every single week. It's the one time per week we ask all of our real estate agents to come into the office. It is highly valuable because we are conducting training, making announcements, and letting them know about changes that are coming up in the market. It is also a chance for us to get face-to-face with our people who are normally working from home or a coffee shop or may be out in a field showing houses. We don't see them on a daily basis. Check in on your folks who are not attending these training meetings. Track attendance at these meetings.

People who do not feel they are part of a team begin to disengage. If you track attendance and you see that somebody has missed two or three weeks in a row, a simple phone call to that person can go a long way. Simply touch base and say, "Hey, we missed you. Hope you are doing okay. I am just checking in to see if there is anything I can do to help you and support you at a higher level than I am currently?"

People who do not feel they are part of a team begin to disengage.

Let's apply this to the church world. I am involved in ministry as well. I have seen people be part of a church for years and years and hardly ever miss outside of illness or emergency. Then somebody is out for three or four weeks in a row and nobody calls to check on them. They may start feeling like they are not valued and may begin thinking that the church does not care about them as much as they thought they did. I've seen people go from church to church or small group to small group looking for that sense of community that they're not getting at their current place of worship.

You should be the same way with your salespeople. Make it a phone call, not a text message. While text messages are great, quick and convenient, taking the time out of your busy schedule to call a sales rep to let them hear your voice and check in on them makes them feel valued and can help them re-engage.

2. Celebrate wins! If someone in your organization has a big sale, has a big week, or closes on a deal, then contact them with either a phone call or a video text. I live on a dirt road out in the country. I walk my dogs a few times per week. While I am walking the dogs, I will send very personalized video text messages. I say their name and celebrate something specifically that they did. They know I'm a busy person and I have a lot on my plate and it means a lot to them when I personally take the time to send them a video text message or simply call them. A quick phone call or video message while you're stuck in traffic or waiting on your order of food goes a long way as well.

3. Schedule monthly one-on-one sessions where you discuss personal life and business life with these folks. Get to know them on a personal level. Figure out what they might be struggling with, not only concerning their business but maybe concerning their health or mindset. Present a growth plan to them. You might lose people because they have reached the top of your organization and there is nowhere higher on your ladder for them to climb. Then they feel it's time to go to another company to get to the next level.

If you have ever studied Maslow's hierarchy of needs, then you have seen the pyramid diagram where people actually value love and belonging, self-esteem, and self-actualization above food, water, and shelter.

People will stay with you for the long haul if they are getting value, love, a sense of belonging, self-esteem and self-actualization. It is easy for people to leave when they don't feel like they are part of your work community. When they see their work as just a job, it is easy to walk away from. But when they feel like they are walking away from their community, away from their people, they almost feel like they are stabbing you in the back because you spent so much time and energy developing them. It is hard for them to walk away in that circumstance. When that recruiter calls from another organization and the salesperson is in a sales slump but they know that their leader has been calling them and has been asking them to come to trainings and one-on-one meetings, it is really hard for that recruiter to get them to leave when you, as their leader, are doing your job.

> *It is easy for people to leave when they don't feel like they are part of your work community.*

Here are a couple of things to think about as we wrap up this chapter. If they are playing for you, they are not playing for someone else. I see a lot of people get rid of low producing individuals because they feel like it hurts their ego. Not everybody has to be a top producer. Should they be trying to get better? Yes. But for me in the real estate industry, if somebody is happy doing real estate part-time and they only sell one house every quarter and they pay their monthly dues on time, that's fine with me. If they are part of our organization and they speak well about our organization, I don't care what their sales states look like.

Be careful about pushing those people to the side. Sometimes you can make even more money over the long haul with those kinds of folks than you can from a top producer for 6 months to a year. Think about the lifetime value of a person staying with you. They might only sell four houses per year but they may introduce you to one of their friends who may come onto your team and that person may become a big time producer for you. You would have never gotten the big time producer if you pushed the lower producer out the door. You don't want to be known as a revolving door type of organization. The easiest way to do this is make your people feel like you care.

Again, remember Maslow's hierarchy of needs. People value love and belonging, self-esteem and self-actualization above food, water, and shelter.

> *People value love and belonging, self-esteem and self-actualization above food, water, and shelter.*

Chapter 9

Scaling the Business

You can build out the best business model, recruit the best people into your organization, help get them into production and have high levels of retention, but can your business scale?

Here is an example of something I did wrong in the beginning when I was growing my real estate company. It didn't scale well for me and I had to fix it.

When I would add real estate agents to my team, they would have to go through four live coaching sessions over a two week period. It took fourteen days for them to get all of the training in. Once they got through the training, there was a skills test at the end of those four sessions. That's how we made sure they knew how to log into their CRM, how to open up a lock box so they could show houses, and they knew how to schedule showings through our showing service. Those four sessions were really the basics of the business. It covered how to generate leads, how to convert at sales appointments, how to write offers on houses and then what to do after their offers got accepted.

It sounds like a pretty good program, right? But what if I had just given class number one on Monday and a new agent joined the team on Tuesday? Do I catch them up in a private session for class one and then add them in with the rest of the group that's onboarding at the same time? What if I had just given class number two on Thursday? Do I catch them up in a private session where I go over class number one and class number two with them one-on-one and then add them in with the rest of the group for sessions three and four? Or do I wait until the next group starts in 2 weeks and possibly lose the momentum of this new hire coming on board? What if somebody wants to join today and go through all four sessions over the next 4 days so they can get out into the field making money sooner? What if I was gone on vacation for a week and nobody was there to train new hires?

You see, I had a problem. It was actually an easy problem to solve. All I had to do was take those four live sessions that I used to give in person and simply record them, break them down into shorter segments. I made an online course that our agents could go through as fast or as slow as they wanted and as many times as they needed to. Problem solved! Right? We were good to go. Or so I thought.

What I really learned is that there were even more questions to be answered and even more support needed once they got out into the field. The online course could not/would not/should not answer every single thing that they're going to encounter when they're out there in the field working with customers. I would get questions like, "Are the closing costs different on a cash sale versus a financed sale?" "I have a full price offer in hand but I have two more showings scheduled today. Should I take the offer that I have or do I wait until after these other showings?"

Read the *New One Minute Manager* by Ken Blanchard and Spencer Johnson. It is a great book out there for all leaders to read. You can better learn how to respond to your employee questions but the bigger question that I would ask you is, why are you the one even taking these questions in the first place? Why was I the bottleneck in this process? All the agents that we hired called me directly. On top of everything else I had going on, I was pausing and disrupting my day to answer simple questions like these. I was basically on call 24/7. That sounds okay when you're small but that certainly does not scale past a certain point. Being on call 24/7 - is this really what you want your life to look like? All questions coming through you all hours of the day, every day? That's not a business, is it?

I want to share with you a foundational business principle that I strongly believe in: you will give up some profit for the sake of scalability. You will lose a little bit of money for the sake of having a business that can scale and go bigger. But if you do this, you will be able to make it up by having a business that can scale and go bigger than what you are personally capable of doing by yourself.

> *You will give up some profit for the sake of scalability.*

Here is an example. In the real estate industry, passive income from recruiting agents to your company is a very popular way for real estate companies to grow their business and for real estate agents to make extra money on top of selling houses. The company pays a portion of revenue that they would not have had to the agent who brings in the new hire. In return, the company gets money that they would not have had. The agent who recruited them gets paid a little bit that they would not have had if this program was not in place and the company gets part of the commission on every closing that that agent has.

There are companies out there that have built their entire platforms around getting their current sales people to recruit new salespeople into the company. Multi-level marketing companies are a very viable and profitable way of doing business. They have been around for years and years and there are people in those models making a ton of money simply by recruiting people into the company.

Knowing this, I took advantage of this opportunity. Our agents typically start at a 70%/30% split. Every time they sell a house, they get 70% of the commission and the company gets 30%. We created a program called "5% For Life" where agents who recruit other agents into the company get a 5% commission override on every sale that comes in from the new hire. 70% still goes to the new agent who sold the house. The company gets 25% instead of 30% and the agent who did the recruiting gets 5%.

For example, on a $6,000 commission check, the agent who recruited that agent gets a $300 recruiting referral fee and that goes on for as long as both agents stay with the company. That is why we call it "5% For Life." It sounds great right? The problem with these models is that most salespeople don't recruit and you really don't want them to recruit. In my opinion, you want them out there selling. These types of programs sound great and it may be a deciding factor whether you join this company versus another company if you have something like this in place but the percentage of salespeople making big money from these recruiting programs is minimal.

Here is what I did. I knew that agents were looking for ways to make money outside of just selling houses so I took my best 70%/30% agents, those who were doing the right things, were good representatives of the company, that showed up for training, and did things the right way, and we started an advisor program with those agents. I would recruit the new agents in and pass them off to an advisor agent. That advisor agent would help them get logged into the online course, administer the skills test when the new hire was ready, and the advisor became the first point of contact for the new hires over the course of their entire career. Instead of me taking all the phone calls, I was spreading that out amongst a team of trained advisors who already had successful experience out in the field. It allowed me to do just one monthly meeting with my advisor team. I would train my advisors and the advisors would train the agents.

Do you see how that is more scalable? It wasn't more profitable because I was giving away part of my 30% to the advisors but consider the amount of time that I saved! Think about what I could have done with that extra time. Could I have recruited more agents knowing that I wasn't going to have to take all those agents' phone calls? Onboarding and training new people is very time consuming if you do it correctly.

I created a more scalable model that wasn't as profitable as the model I had before. We eventually made it more profitable because we could bring in a lot more people by doing it this way versus everybody having to come to me.

We developed these advisors into leaders through this process. A few of them went on to start their own real estate teams within our office. Some of those teams got big enough where they branched out and opened up their own offices. That was one of the ways I was able to quickly expand and go from one location to 10 locations. Some of the people that I brought in on the 70%/30% model eventually became advisors, then became team leaders and then franchisees.

Think about this from the advisor standpoint. If you've got a salesperson who is making $1,000 a month in passive monthly income from recruiting referrals. They are not leaving when that recruiter calls trying to get them to come across town to go to that other company. They would be walking away from an easy monthly payday. They didn't recruit these people in because I was the recruiter. They just trained the ones that I brought in for them and I gave them the "5% For Life." I decided that I was going to build their downlines for them. It was

> *I was going to make my model more profitable and, in the meantime, recruiting went up, retention went up, and scalability went up.*

going to make my model more profitable and, in the meantime, recruiting went up, retention went up, and scalability went up.

Chapter 10

What's Next?

What do you do when you find yourself in a place where you truly own a business? Your business is running without you, operating with very little of your daily input and hardly takes up any of your time. What's next? Unfortunately, I cannot give an exact answer because I don't know what you are into but the general answer is, whatever you want!

You may decide that you like this gig of being an entrepreneur and you want to keep growing. You might want to get bigger and add more locations. You may decide you want to open more locations. You might look into franchising or trademarking or your own corporate stores where you are 100% owner.

For me, once I got a real estate team that had several agents with a plethora of sales, it made sense for me to open up a title company I could utilize to close all of those sales. When you have a large team that is closing a lot of deals, you can get in the room and start having those types of conversations.

Now, I don't know the first thing about running a title company. I wouldn't even know where to start. I'm going to suggest that as you look at these new venture possibilities, you don't try to bet on yourself and do all the work yourself, like many of you did to get this first business up and going. You worked so hard to get yourself out of having a job. Let's guard our time and energy by not jumping back into another thing that is going to take up more of your time and energy.

> *Let's guard our time and energy by not jumping back into another thing that is going to take up more of your time and energy.*

When I opened up a title company, it was as simple as finding a title company that was already in operation that already had people hired and had the technology and insurance needed. They already had the legal background and the infrastructure in place. They were wanting to grow their business and did not have a location where I was located. I went in together as a partner and we formed a joint venture where we were 50/50 owners. They ran everything and staffed everything. My part of the partnership was to simply get our agents to use the title company as much as we could control (which has some limitations) but it was a very minimal amount of extra work for me.

I would get a profit and loss statement every month that showed how much money came in and the expenses for running the branch. Most of the employees were in a back office somewhere, working remotely, already hired and already trained. The bottom line was how much profit we made per month. 10% went into savings and we would 50/50 the rest.

How many of those types of businesses could you have open if you were not the one running it every day? How many more locations could you open if you found a company like that that wanted to grow? What if you could figure out areas where they could expand to and you simply put the deal together and get an even smaller percentage? Could you find a real estate team somewhere where that particular title company is not currently located and introduce them to each other in exchange for 5% to 10% ownership? They're doing all the work. You're just putting the deal together. This is key! These are the kinds of things that you need to start looking for when considering your next steps.

Once you have unloaded the day-to-day responsibilities of this business from your plate you may find yourself, as Coach Micheal Burt says, a level 10 person at a level four opportunity. You may find that the amount of time and energy that you invested into this one business pales in comparison to other opportunities that you have found out there. That is completely okay.

I am not a big fan of shutting down businesses that are making profits every month but you may decide to shift your energy into something that is more profitable. Keep this level four business open while you go out and explore the level 10 opportunities.

I have a Google Drive spreadsheet that I track all of my monthly income sources on a month-to-month basis between the 5th and the 10th of every month. I look at disbursements that I have received from businesses that I own and businesses where I am a part owner. I compare those numbers to what they were a year ago, a month ago, and last quarter. Sometimes we have to shut down the businesses that are not making money or those that are declining in performance. There is a game you have to play.

I encourage you to be very careful about avoiding the temptation to jump back in and grow something yourself the way you did for the first business. You have worked all this time to get yourself unstuck. Let's not get ourselves stuck ever again. Let's get unstuck for life.

You have worked all this time to get unstuck. Let's not get ourselves stuck ever again. Let's get unstuck for life.

If there is anything I can do to help you get unstuck, feel free to reach out. I would love to connect with you. Thank you for reading this book. I hope it has been a help to you. I would love to hear how this book has affected you and your business.